THE POWER OF DETERMINATION

Train Your Mind to Live Your Calling

LUSENE DONZO

ISBN: 979-8-6390-2221-0

To my mother Clara, I am grateful for everything you taught me as a man. I wouldn't be the man I am today if it was not for you.

Dad, thank you for telling me to read The Magic of Thinking Big *by David Swartz. That book changed my life.*

Uncle Kalilu, thank you for everything you did for me. It motivated to become a person of influence

My brothers and sister, being the oldest, was the best thing that could ever happen to me in this life.

To the thousands of individuals reading this book. Thank you for taking your time to read this book.

CONTENTS

LUSENE DONZO

###

INTRODUCTION

"Your service to others is the rent that you pay while you are on earth."

--Mohammed Ali

"Your time is limited, so do not waste it living someone else's life."

--Steve Jobs

"My mother used to tell me that man gives you award, but God gives you reward"

--Denzel Washington

I remember when I woke up in the hospital.

Everyone was staring down at me. I could not help but ask myself, how did I bring myself to be in the predicament that I was in. My mom was right by my side, along with friends and family. I was supposed to be unstoppable. Before that experience, I have never been at the hospital for anything serious. I was supposed to be going into my senior year of college. Being in the best shape of my life both physically, mentally and spiritually fit.

When the doctor approached me, the very first thing he said was this, "You are fortunate to be alive, young man." To be honest, I did not understand the magnitude of what he said until I spent the next several days going through surgeries, just to get back to my usual self. At that moment I realized that it's a privilege to be alive after having two seizures in one day. Most people might not look at it as anything, but I looked at it as if God had a purpose for me to be on this earth still.

I spent about five days in that hospital, the first three days, I had the catheter attached to my private part. That was the most intriguing part because prior to this incident I was so arrogant. I was very selfish and not humble at all. Sometimes you must be broken to get to where you need to go. After a couple days I tried to get up, I was having a hard time. I could barely feed myself because my shoulders felt like I was carrying about 80 pounds on each of them. I cried multiple times, while I was in the hospital. I was devastated with myself, I hated myself so much for putting us in the predicament.

The thought of me not doing anything for myself fueled me. So then I decided, whenever I get out of this situation and graduate college, I will spend the rest of my life doing all the things that I ever wanted to do. I realized that I had lived my life in fear, people pleasing, selfishness and that was not who I was from the core. I had lost my true self. I had lost what I stood for. I had lost what I wanted to be because I care about what other people thought about me. I had lost one of the most important things we all have, which is our gift.

You see it took me to have a near death situation just to understand how valuable my life is. This does not have to be you. If you are reading this book, please understand that you already have all that you need to become successful. I would tell you to take some notes of some of the things that resonate with you. A lot of people doubted my potential and did not think I could do what I am doing but that is the beauty of life. We are all meant to transform and evolve into our true self, through struggles and setbacks.

Finally, what I recommend to you is either something that I have done, or I am currently doing. Just remember that nothing is impossible on this earth. Always be an open-minded person when it comes to knowledge.

Take a deep breath and let me explain to you my story and why you should follow your dreams and train your mind to live your calling. It's time to take a chance on your dream and break out of the rat race.

PILLAR #1

Chapter 1

GIVE YOUR DREAMS A CHANCE

Growing up in Monrovia, Liberia, adults would talk about America like it was heaven, and if you were to ever go there, you could make all your dreams possible. Ever since I heard those words as a kid, it always resonates to me that only in America could I accomplish all my dreams if I was to go there.. I was very interested and made it a goal of mine to go to America. I remember that at one point in my life it became an obsession. I made it a purpose as a child if I were to ever have an opportunity to come. I would take advantage of it! Growing up in several countries in West African humbled me. Being born in American is a huge blessing for some of us, compared to being born in a third world country. Things like Medicaid, child support, food stamps, free school systems, were not available during the time I was growing up. There is a vast significant gap between American and some of the countries that I grew up in back home, which is why I am so passionate about living out my calling. I made a declaration to myself that as a child when I come to America, I will make every one of my dreams become a reality.

Your dreams and imaginations are everything in this world. If you genuinely want to become a better you, you must learn how to use them to become better. We all have the ambition and vision to make our dreams become a reality, but most times, we refuse to use our imagination. You are never really going to accomplish the things that you want if you do not imagine it happening to you. You need to believe in yourself. The best part of your life lies in your dream, and I believe that your real success lies in your dreams and goals. If you are not willing to sacrifice going to the next level to make your dream become a reality, you are selling yourself short. I realized at a young age that my dreams were not just about me, especially when I decided to join the military. I realized that being in the service was something bigger than myself. After joining the service, I also decided to follow my other dream of becoming a Professional Speaker.

We all have a gift from God. Whether that is singing, being an athlete, etc. Everyone on this earth can be inspired by what you are going to create. We are all connected in this life. We need each other, and our dream can influence and have positive effects on others. Your dream is something that every individual in this world could benefit from. You must rise and say, "I am taking control over my life, and chase all my dreams and goals." So, continue to grind towards your dream with a passion. Only in your passion, I believe, lies your most significant opportunity for success.

Do you believe that following your calling is worth it? Naturally, it is, you see, following a calling no matter whether you reached it or now will help develop you in every aspect of your life from personal to career. As I stated earlier, your dream is your vision; it is something that pulls you closer to something you were destined for. However, if you do so, follow your calling, make sure it is something that you can achieve by working hard because I can almost guarantee you that it will be worth it in the end. Your calling is something that is going to excite you. It is something more breathtaking, especially when you are at the moment. You might think you don't feel like you deserve it, or you might not be worthy. You might even have a fear of failure, which I had several years ago. It is okay to fear failure. We all are afraid of something, which is what makes us human. Although, you will need to address your fears head-on and continue to follow your heart desire and believe in yourself. I promise you will achieve your dreams after overcoming your fear.

Is it worth it to risk it all for your calling? I do not think it's in good interest for everyone to risk everything just to follow their calling, but I do believe that God works magically and what might work for John might not work for Lisa, as we all have different journeys and struggles that we must go through. I remember when I had my seizure and the Doctor told me that I must stay on the medication for about two years, and I would not be able to drive. It was very tough, I was devastated because I had never had a seizure in my life before. I realized that I could sit there and listen to what the Doctor had to say and believe everything or refuse the situation to cloud my judgment. I decided that I was going to risk it because accomplishing my dreams and goals were more important than settling for the life I was given. I refused to stay on the medication for the rest of my life and not being able to drive myself. I had worked too hard to where I had come from. I picture all the kids from African depending on me. We focus a lot of energy on a problem, instead of seeking a solution. Whatever problem that you are going through in your life right now is always going to be a problem if you do not think of a solution. So, I asked the Doctor how I can get off the medication slowly because I knew I needed it at the moment, but I did not want to get off completely. He advised me otherwise, but I told him I was willing to gamble because I refused to live the rest of my life on medication. The Doctor did not diagnose me with Epilepsy. Maybe you are going through a life-changing event that I went through, or stuck in a relationship that you do not want to be in, and your heart is telling you otherwise. I would say to you to listen to what you truly believe in. You see, I knew the consequences of the seizure medication, and I was willing to bet that I rather worked to get off then stay on it for two years. The drug was making me lose my hair, my memory. I took a considerable risk with my life but as the old saying goes "Without risk there is no reward."

Will you be able to handle your calling? Well, you will never know until you execute. I have come to realize in my young life that God would not give me more than I could handle. But the hope that I will be speaking in front of thousands of people makes me have enough faith that he would always look out for me no matter the obstacles. For instance, sometimes you can plan your life and push yourself to follow your calling but still do not end up accomplishing anything. Here's the key, do not focus on what you will stumble on right now, but focus on what you could become. See your potential on the inside every day that you are living. I understand that sometimes you might want to do something, but someone close to you might tell you otherwise like "You are crazy, you are never going to accomplish that." The best advice anyone ever told me when it came to my dream was what my best friend told me when I told her about being a Professional Speaker "She said Lusene, you always get excited about doing something and being a Professional Speaker is just another one of your talks." Little did she know that she inspired me because she was right. All I did was talk about speaking but I never actually decided to execute it. I quickly realized that I had to act on my dreams because nobody was going to act on it for me.

You want your life to be the way you want it, how you want it and live where you want, all that is possible, but you have got to understand mother nature will not give you precisely what you want if you are not willing to put in the work. Following your calling is going to be twists and turns.. It is like running, most kids growing up naturally do not like running, but as they continue to do it and find out they are good at it. They will eventually end up being good which results in them being a professional athlete or they would just run for fun. Every runner knows that the best satisfaction about running is reaching your destination. It's your experiences that you have gained and learned from life that will help you along your journey while you are following your dream.

Don't let anyone stop you from believing that you can accomplish your dreams and goals. Colonel Sanders opened the first Kentucky Fried Chicken restaurant when he was 62 old! I do not think anyone believed he could do it, but he did. He never gave up. The difficulties you are going through right now are going to help you become the person you need to be later; so, appreciate life. Life will have a series of setbacks, but setbacks are temporary. A lot of people have made a comeback from tragedy and you are not an exception. Depending on what stage you are in your life, you may have had a lot of setbacks! Although there is no way, you will leave this world without going through something disappointing. Decide today to follow your dream because the world is counting on you to make a difference!

Chapter 2

I AM AN INSPIRATION

John Quincy Adams once said, "If your action inspires others to dream more, learn more and do more than become more; you are a leader."

Being the oldest of five kids is not something I can truly say has been easy. My parents have always set a high expectation for me. Sometimes I used to wonder why they were so hard on me. I remember when I came from Guinea I did not know how to speak English correctly. My father homeschools me for a very long time. During my time in Ivory Coast, my Dad used to always make me read self-improvement books such as Rich Dad Poor Dad. I hated reading at the time. All I wanted to do was to go outside and play with my friends. My father will always tell me that I was great and it was his job to install the fundamentals in me. He will regularly remind me that I am his oldest son and that I represent him, my mother and my younger siblings. I did not care because all I wanted to do was play with my friends and be like a regular kid. I now love reading and I have read Rich Dad Poor Dad numerous times to grasp the concept. It was not until when I came to America, I realized that my father was helping me to become an independent man by making me understand that reading is going to be one of my fundamentals of success. I always admired the fact that no matter where I went in the Ivory Coast everyone knew about my dad and would say a tremendous thing about the type of man he was. I do not have the best relationship with my father, but I would say he had a somewhat positive inspiration in my life. My father inspired me to always work on my dreams and goals.

Everyone that ever took a chance at pursuing something that they believe in regardless of the circumstances is leaders. Leaders take the risk that the rest of individuals don't want to take, understanding that they have got to set an example for their company, business or everyone else. When people doubt their ability to see beyond their circumstances, they are at right now and just settle for life. They will tell you about what you intend to do is impossible. Do not listen to those types of individuals because I would say success is doing the little things each day to get the results. When I decided I wanted to become a Professional Speaker; I quickly realized that I had to learn how to read and write better. I mentioned early that I hated reading earlier because my father would make me read books that I did not understand at the time. I decided to give reading a chance again because I was not reading for myself, but I was reading for the sake of knowledge and information. We all know that information changes the situation, and if you want to change any situation, you are in for the better you have got to educate yourself.

Earlier last year I was listening to one of Les Brown's speeches and he said, "If you do what is easy your life will be hard, but if you do what is hard then your life will be easy." When I first heard this quote, I was in total disarray because I did not understand what it meant. Maybe you are going through hardships right now, and your life is hard. You keep putting in the work to become a better athlete, but you see no results; you keep taking a chance on chasing your dreams, but nobody is given you any chances or opportunity or you are living out of your vehicle just to get by to pursue your dreams. Some of you might be working a full-time job while putting in working overtime on your dreams. Regardless of what you are going through, always remember that you can be an inspiration to somebody one day or you are an inspiration to someone, but you should never give up no matter how hard the road is. Life is going to be hard anyway when you are doing something that the average person does not do. There have been numerous times in my life where I felt like quitting and giving up, although I always will remember that I am the oldest of 5 kids and my brothers and sister are looking up to me.

When someone asks me the question of what is one word that describes you, I always use the word "Inspire." I have always thought of being an inspiration to the world, I want to get to a point where I can affect so many people in this world positively. One of the first things I asked myself was how I was going to do that. I consistently searched for those answers throughout all my years in college, but I did not find it until I had my seizure and I started reading and educating myself. To me, self-learning is one of the most excellent tools a person can have. In any skill set self-learning requires you to learn things and master it on your own or you could seek other's help. This is very important when it comes to following your dreams because each and everyone in this world has different gifts and dreams and it is up to you to self-educate yourself in that area. Warren Buffett said it the best "The best investment you can make is an investment in yourself, the more you learn, the more you earn." I realized that if I wanted to inspire people in this world, I would have to invest in myself continually, do things that I do not want to do, but I know that it's for the best. When you are following your dreams, please understand that you are leaving a trail for someone else to replicate what you did or do it even better. The point of human life is for us to continuously get better because only are you truly living when you are challenging yourself and putting yourself through things that will benefit not only you but for the wellbeing of others.

The beautiful thing about being an inspiration is we must realize that we are a gift from God. So, my question to you is that if you are doing what you love or have found out what it is that you love. Don't you think you deserve to be doing what you love for the rest of your life regardless of whether there is money involved in it or not? I believe that if you do what you love and continue to work on your skills; you can figure out how to make money doing it. The problem with us today is that we appreciate it when a different individual is creative, selfless, innovative, or dare to be different. We think that they are different from us. What makes people like Michael Jordan, Martin Luther King, and Lebron James different from you. They are all ordinary people who decided that the world needed to know their gifts, and they were bold enough to follow their dreams and become an inspiration. A true leader believes that they could change the world despite all the odds that are against them, but most importantly, they were not afraid to try.

Too many of us have failed to see the greatness in ourselves. You can look at someone that is struggling through life right now and tell him that everything is going to be okay and he should have faith; I can almost guarantee that he would not agree with you because the problem with society today is that when we struggle that is all we see. You have got to learn to see past through your struggle and see through your greatness, but most importantly your potential. There is another skeptic that we believe that a person is only great if they make national headlines or are on television. You see the press does not need to know you are doing something inspirational. I firmly believe that the most inspirational people go unnoticed all the time. It's okay if you do go unnoticed, but the point of being an inspiration is to know that you have done something to make better humanity or your area of interest. It is a great feeling to see how you have made others feel when you have achieved your dreams.

The individuals who have had the most significant impact on my life are the ones that have had a challenging experience but overcome the challenges life continues to throw at them. Although however, they continued to make a difference with a smile on their face, no matter how big or small it might be. Life is going to be hard, but that does not mean that it is impossible. You must make a declaration to yourself to keep fighting for your dream regardless of the circumstances life throws at you. However, when you limit your ability to become successful because of your situation, that will become your imagination, and you will not succeed. As you wake up to embark on your journey of chasing your dream and becoming an inspiration, you will notice that every day will not be a good day but there is a good in every single day depending on how you could look at it. You are here because of you and you are the only person that can get yourself out of the situation. Do not get hung up on who does and does not support your dream. As you support your dream, that is all that matters. My mother always used to say, "every day above ground is a day to give grace to God." If you do not go after what you want, you will never have it, stop waiting for the perfect time or moment and DO IT NOW. Never forget the point of life is to find your voice or dream so that you can make it, and when you get there, you can encourage someone else to follow theirs.

Chapter 3

NOBODY WILL DO IT FOR YOU

Real success is not free, you will have to put in the work. Would you not be happy if you tried and succeeded? I can guarantee you that it would be well worth it. Learning to embrace adversity when you are under pressure, helps you build confidence, which will enable you to reach higher toward the life that you would want. There is nothing in this life that God is not going to pull you through, maybe he is currently pulling you through something now.

You see, I joined the Army to overcome my fear of change, but I decided to become a Military Officer because I wanted to be responsible for other people. I love the fact that the Army is a very challenging job, but it has taught me one of the most valuable leadership skills that I used today in my life. The minute your life is falling apart, and you do not know what there is to do; I need you to understand that you can sit there and let life run through you or you can get up and take responsibility for your life and dreams. I remembered that I worked hard in ROTC to get an Active Duty slot, and when I finally got it I was happy, but I almost lost everything. However, I refused to quit and give in because I knew that nobody was going to make my dream of becoming a Military Officer and Professional Speaker a reality. That moment when things are bad do not play the victims and crawl into a corner. It is the time for you to look at your dreams. This is your opportunity to see just how much you have learned from what it is that you have been through previously.

I live my life, expecting good things to happen to me. I am always looking for an opportunity. I live my life understanding that I will fail my way to success. I have become so obsessed with failing that it does not bother me anymore because I know every failure is a lesson and one step closer to my dreams. For the past several years, I have learned that failing, training, and managing your thoughts is an essential skill that you can do when it comes to you being successful.

Every day when I wake up, I make it my duty to read my dreams out loud and say several affirmations. I have come to realize that what I dream about is only a fraction of what it takes to accomplish my dream. The goals that I have read to myself is just the beginning of the dream. If you live the life that you want and be part of the extraordinary individual in this world, you will have to be willing to sacrifice and put in the work. Take a moment to find out what you want to do. I will be honest when you start developing yourself to become the person that you need for you to become who you are meant to me. It is one of the best feelings in the world. Life does not matter what other people think of you. The best person you can ever be in this world is yourself, and if you love yourself enough to overcome your fear and then step into the life you want. Although sometimes you may not know that your journey will bring you into your dreams, be open-minded, enjoy your process, and always remember to seize the opportunity that God brings to you.

When life is throwing things at you, get your plan together that you have had, and commit to working continuously towards your dream. I said early that my mother was a very hard-working woman. She would always tell me not to ever give up on anything and to continue praying and working hard. Eventually, I will achieve the results. So why should you keep working towards your dreams. Well, if you do not work towards it, you will never accomplish it. But however, if you continue to take a stab at your dreams and goals each day, eventually something gotta give!

One of the most important decisions you will make each day is what you will do when you wake up. That is going to help you towards your dream and how far would you push it later. Failure to do that is one of the most crucial reasons individuals do not become who they said they were going to be. Realize that your decision to continuously work on a specific plan that pertains to your dream no matter how small it is can be a huge benefit when it comes to making it a reality versus you not doing anything at all. I have realized that part of my success is tackling my morning. Earlier in my life, I talked about how writing down my goals helped me achieve a lot of things that I wanted to do; I also had a clearer vision. Planning out your days does the same thing but, it's way more effective in my opinion because when you put the smaller pieces together, only then you will be able to see the big picture. For you to go up any stairs, you have got to start with the first stair. You cannot get to the top just like that, you will have to step on a couple of stairs before you reach the top. Same applies to your dreams. When you plan out your day and do the things that pertain to you and to get better continuously. You gave yourself a sense of purpose and vision for that day. One of the reasons I love the military is that we have a training schedule of about 90-180 plans, and every week we review it to make sure we are either going according to the training schedule or other things that take more priority than some of the things on the calendar. Stop waking up in the morning with no plan. Come up with a strategy that is going to help you to become great at whatever it is that you want to do.

Some of you want to become a politician, actress, actor, professional athlete, but you do not have a strategy of getting to your destination. I need you to become strategic when it comes to having the life that you want because nobody will do it for you. I realize that on the days I failed to be productive is when I have no sense of purpose. I go through my days doing what I can, and I am not working toward anything. Your strength is in your routine. Wake up in the morning looking at your dreams, always think of how you can accomplish, continuously act on it, make sure that you are taking care of yourself physically, and eating the proper nutrition to sustain your body. One of the things that we failed to realize is that the body we have will be with us until the day we die, so you might as well take care of it. Most importantly, getting the right amount of sleep is an essential part of your morning routine. Part of the reason a lot of people struggle to acquire the life that they want is that they do not have a morning routine. However, if you do have a routine, please continue to stick to that routine that is helping you to progress. The great things in life are not going to come easy to you, so you have got to find them. When you are bold enough to take a chance on your dreams, eventually you are going to soar and accomplish them. When I got to the point where all I wanted to do was to be successful, I was willing to stay committed to achieving everything that I want. I have always had a strong work ethic, but I never had anything that I was passionate about and not become committed. When you get to a point in your life where your success is more important, and you do not care about failing in the directions that you want to go, that is when you will be successful.

Chapter 4

EVERYDAY YOU ARE DYING

After going to see my neurologist several times when I had a seizure, I had one more appointment before he could make a final decision on whether I could commission as an Officer.

I was nervous. It was an emotional morning for me because everything I ever worked for in the Reserve Officer Training Corps had come down to this moment. I felt awful as I was driving. I am a person that believes in hard work. I believe that if you work hard to get something and you earn it, it is a great accomplishment. I was struggling financially, my roommate was taking care of my share of rent and paying some of my bills. Suddenly, I recalled that through everything that I have gone through I have always expected good things to happen to me regardless of the circumstances. I also remembered that I had faith in God that I was going to be okay when I was going through my surgeries when I had a seizure. I remembered to recycle my pain. So, as I got out of the car, I kept the same faith I had when I was hospitalizing and that everything was going to be okay. As I have always stated that my mother has always been an inspiration, although we do not agree on a lot of things, one thing I do love about my mother is that she works hard and has tremendous faith in God. I watched my mother work to provide for us when I was younger, and even when I came back to live with her after high school.

I know that with everything in my life that God is always going to do what is best for me, regardless if I do not see it. I will become someone great due to being cut from a different cloth. I do not think God took me from Ivory Coast to live in America to just be average. Through all the struggles I went through, I realized that my purpose is greater than the pain I have to go through. I firmly believe that everything that happens is meant to make or break you depending on how you look at it. As I walked out of my car, to head over to the counter I told the lady I am here to see my neurologist. I ended up signing some paper and went to see the Nurse. She was going to check my blood pressure and do the necessary things that they do when you come to visit a specialist.

In life, some people you meet will forever have an impact on your life because of the things they say or tell you. It can either be positive or negative. I tend to always have a conversation with everybody that I come across. My goals are to either learn something from them, or they learn something from me. So, I began to engage in the conversation with the Nurse; I proceeded in asking her age. She was about 60+ years old and was still working. So, I asked her how long she has been working as a Nurse, she told me about 40 years. I was shocked because I would not be wanting to work for 40 years. Then I proceeded in asking her if she loves what she does, she told me that, not only she loves what she does, but being a Nurse was her calling and her destined job, and she wouldn't trade it for anything in this world. I was very shocked at how this old lady was passionate about being a nurse. She later asked me why I am so interested in her. I told her that I am just lost, and I am trying to find my purpose in life, but I want to do something that I am in love with. That was when she told me something that changed my life. She said, "From the day you came out of your mother's womb as a baby, you are dying. So, if you live life understanding you are closer to your death, you will spend less time on doing things you know that you really do not want to do. She later said, "that she will continue to become a Nurse until the day she cannot perform her job anymore."

Often people will always try to find blame on why they are not doing what they love or why they are not happy. They will say things like God does not love me, I cannot find a job, nobody wants to hire me. When I was a freshman in college I struggled to find work; I wanted to work so much, but I failed to realize that there is a time for everything. Most of the time, everything in your life comes at the time you need it to arrive. In this life, there is only one thing that is certain, which is death. There is an old saying that says nobody in this world is going to make it out alive. Which is the truth, because when you realize that eventually you are going to die, whether that is sooner or later. Your perspective about your dreams will change. When you know that you are going to die regardless of what you are doing, only then will you ask yourself the tough questions of what are the things I would love to do before it's my time to go. How do I want to remember, what do I want my legacy to be?

Aside from death, what is it that you want to accomplish on this earth. What skills are you willing to gain and attain to live that life that you want. What jobs are you willing to work, what friends are you ready to obtain or sacrifice, how far are you willing to work every Saturday and Sunday, just to accomplish the desired life that you want. To be honest, one of my greatest fears in life, is to not live a life doing something that I am not in love with. As I stated, I love being a soldier and I would never trade it for anything in the world because the military has made a tremendous difference in my life. I met my two-best friend in the military. Even when I do get out of the military or retire I will always be a soldier but as I stated previously. However, my dream is and will always be to become a Public Speaker.

After that Nurse left, I felt slightly hopeful that regardless of what the Doctor says, I will be okay. I trusted in God's steps for my life. You see regardless whether I was going to be commissioned as a military officer. I have always been ambitious and expected great things from myself, and I was willing to put in the work to become great. God cannot bless your steps if you are not taking any. Some of you don't realize that the reason why you have not reached the level that you wanted to reach is because you have not taken the necessary step to get to where you need to be. I firmly believe in believing before you see it happens.

Nobody believed in my dreams of becoming a speaker. Nobody understood that I am obsessed with becoming one. I did not have enough money to go to the conference, and I did not know where to start. I was spending so much time trying to figure out how I was going to become a speaker when I neglected the fact that I had to create my opportunities. Most of the time, the things we go to study in college are most likely not our calling or our gift, but it is meant to help us to become the type of person we were meant to become. I was a computer science major trying to become a public speaker. I had never spoken publicly before, but I firmly believe that I had to start somewhere. I kept my head up and continued to face whatever adversity I had to go through. One thing that I learned early in my young life is to never give up on anything that you want to do. I always tell myself that I will never give up and keep believing, having faith, but most importantly, do not let anyone outwork you. Even though I was broke, I realize that I had the greatest gift we all were born with, but neglect to use over the course of our life is our mind.

When you are little, you are told to use your imagination to solve a problem, but as you get older, we start to use it less. Often when there is a problem in our life instead of using our mind to solve it, and figure out how we are going to get out of it, or how we can change it, we play the blame game. Often life is a series of lessons learned and failure overcome. So, therefore, I refuse to think that anything that will ever transpire in my life will be final, and continue to strive towards the life that I want to live. When you embrace your problems and struggle, you will learn something valuable. When life puts you in a dark place or when you are going through your raining season, please understand that it is temporary.

You do not know exactly where your journey is going to take you as you continue to live this life. If you would have told me I would be an Army Officer, I would have told you that it was a lie. Even if you would have told me that I would become a Soldier, I would have argued, but I realized that you have to be open to the process and be open to the steps that will bring you closer to your dream. Never forget to create or seize the opportunities that God or life presents to you, even if they do not seem to fit the path of your dream.

The first tragic event that happened in my life was when my uncle kicked me out of his house the night before my high school graduation and I still went ahead and graduated. My uncle was expecting me to beg him for forgiveness, but I had another mission in my mind which was to graduate. I was on the bus to my grandmother's house and on to my graduation. When you realize that another person's opinion of you does not matter, or no matter what circumstances that life gives you, only you can get yourself out of that situation and into the direction only then you will realize that all things are possible if you believe.

On that day I realized that I could do anything that I wanted to do, I just needed to find the right individual or be surrounded by individuals that are going to help me get to my destination. I needed that event to happen in my life to make me the individual that I am today. Maybe you grew up in a broken home like me, have an abusive guardian, or even lost your parents. Tragedy in life happens, but only in those moments can you realize your true potential. I am not saying that a loved one dying is a good thing, but I firmly believe that all things work together for good. It is part of the process in your life.

One of the things I take pride in is using my imagination when things get tough and my back against the wall. A lot of time, the vision that we have for our life is something that only we can comprehend, and it is beyond our imagination. You cannot allow anybody to kill your creativity because you cannot expect others to see what you believe. The older I am getting, I do not even tell some of my friends my dreams and goals because I feel that I have outgrown them when it comes to being ambitious. You cannot be afraid to spread your dreams and goals because someone else close to you tried and failed. Your true gift is beyond your comfort zone. I will never forget one of the Colonel told us that "You have got to get comfortable, being uncomfortable." To this day I embodied that quote and used it when it comes to following my dreams. A lot of the things that are happening in my life, I never imagined, when I was living in Nzerekore, Guinea.

I have come a long way, I decided to continue to take a chance on myself. When God presents you an opportunity to better yourself, please understand that is your opportunity to use your gift and follow your dreams. I believe that everyone should use their gifts to empower the people around them to do the same with their gifts. Understanding that you do not need to live toward anyone's expectations. It is okay to change for the good because in this life we are living, you came alone in this world and you are going to die alone. The better you become in this world, the more people you will lose because you guys will not have the same perspective. While you embark on your journey, do not be afraid to let go of some of your friends on the way to the top.

PILLAR #2

Chapter 5

IF YOU FAIL TO PLAN, YOU PLAN TO FAIL

I never understood what that quote represents until I met Mr. Mason and he told me about writing down my goals. Ever since then, every conversation we had, he would always tell me about his plan and what he plans on doing with his life and the amount of wealth he hopes to attain at a certain age. We would have multiple conversations about the art of planning your life and he also told me numerous books and ways that I could figure out how to plan my life. My experience in life has taught me that you are going to have challenges in your life. You are either going to be going in a storm, coming out of a storm, or in a storm. However, you cannot let the trials and tribulations consume who you are as an individual. There is a lot of hope to focus on when you know what your dreams are. When you are on your journey to planning your life and your dream, you must let all the negative people go. I have realized that you cannot change the people that you grew up with, or your friends. However, please understand that each one of us was born to be successful, and the journey is not going to be easy.

Your dream is going to become a reality, yes it may not happen in about six months, one year or two years or even more than that, however, if you visualize your life and continue to trust your process, I believe you can make anything become a reality. There is a vast difference between sight and vision to me, and you must be very careful as only one of those words can take you to the promised land. Sight is for individuals that live in the present. Those individuals that believe in sights, must see it before they can do anything or believe it. Although Visionaries are wise because they understand that success will eventually come, seek them, because they have made it their mission to make it happen before it even happens. Visionary knows that their dreams are going to be possible. They have affirmation each day when they wake up. I realized that my life was not going the way I wanted, so I decided to change. I decided to take a chance on my dreams. Some of us get paid to forget our dream, but I say unto you that, no matter what jobs you have never become okay with getting paid to forget your dreams. You must live up and withstand whatever comes in your way. To accomplish your dreams, you must stay hungry.

When we think about what it means to plan your life. Most of us do not think about a plan that includes our dreams, or we do not incorporate it in our plan because it is not ideal. Our mind is a beautiful thing but most of us do not use it. There is no short cut to success. You must realize that you must plan your life regardless whether you are going through the pain or not. Planning and execution go hand in hand. It is easy to plan things in our life and execute it when everything is going right. However, the true purpose of life is to continue to believe in yourself and never settle for the life that you want. When you are going through tragedy and having unexpected things happen to you, always remember that your dreams are waiting for you. Some dreams are in you, it is your time to keep persevering and have the right attitude. Maybe you are going through a difficult time? You have experienced a lot of disappointment. You did not get that promotion that you wanted, you lost your spouse, you got kicked out of college, you did not graduate high school, or you lost a family member. I want you to keep going full throttle at your dreams. It is possible to accomplish whatever we want to achieve in this world. You must understand that in our place of darkness, are our dreams, goals, talents, potential that will only come to life in a dark place. Almost every person who did something great went through a place of darkness. You may not realize it but it's only in the dark place that you are really growing. The dark areas are your prerequisite for stepping into the fullness of your destiny and it is a prerequisite for us as well.

It's the same when you are going through pain of losing a loved one, your spouse divorced you, you have gotten some form of sickness like cancer, you lost your job, and you did not get the promotion that you need. I will say that you have got to trust your process, even in the tough times, when you are hurting the most. You might feel lonely that nobody loves you, and it does not make sense because you are a great person. You consistently catch yourself looking at the ceiling, asking God why ME? And trying to figure out stuff and to make sense of the situation. I will say stop trying to make sense of the situation. There are certain things that are inevitable. God does not make mistakes when it comes to your life.

When you are born in this world, we are all given a life to live but it is up to us for us to create the lifestyle that we want. A lot of time it is easy for us to watch other people that have taken the chance to create the lifestyle that they want. I do not believe anybody in this world became successful by accident. I firmly believe they plan every step of the way and believe that they could do it and then keep on working toward it to make it become a reality. It was not an accident for me to come in American as a refugee. I came into America as a refugee because that was the way God wanted it to be. I had my grandmother and other families that I could have brought me here but my destiny was to come as a refugee in America. You see if I would have come in this country by someone adopting me instead of me coming with my mother as a refugee and us struggling, my course of life, of course would have been way different.

We must have fun planning our dreams. We must decide to continue to get better every single day on the day that we do not feel like it. It is easier to sit and make excuses why we cannot do what we want to do. As the old saying goes. Everyone encounters difficulties, loss, pain, and struggle. Don't give yourself an escape. We all go through hard times, and there were many times in my life I wanted to commit suicide when I was younger, but I am here today because my purpose is bigger than me. I have realized that I will continue to take ownership of my mistakes, problems, future and of my life. I am committed to lead myself to become the person I want to be. There is a purpose in your pain. If you always tend to focus on the present, you will surely get discouraged and think this is not where you are supposed to be. I remember during times of difficulties I only thought about the present, and that almost cost me my life and I would not be here today. I kept on looking into the future and kept on pressing. I kept on embracing my faith and believe that I will get to the success that I want. Yes, I understand, it is going to be difficult, it is not what you planned but understand that this pain is not here to defeat you. This pain is here to push you to the next level of your process. When you have a plan for your dreams, and you are going on that road, it exposes you to a different circumstance and makes you better.

When your plan is not going the way, you want it to go, you cannot get discouraged. Keep going and embrace your struggles because it's going to bring forth something new. You must become uncomfortable during your time of struggles. Keep looking for opportunities. Your struggles are going to help you become successful and help others along with their dreams. Keep focusing on what you must do to get to the next level. When you make your plan, you must see it even if nobody sees it. Every day you must incorporate your plan into your way of life. It must become somewhat of an obsession. You must decide to step into your fears. We get a significant push to work hard from the belief that we are working for something bigger than ourselves. When you decide to keep persevering on your dreams and ideas, you develop trust with yourself. Which then gives you the energy that excites you and inspires you to continue. You must enjoy hitting the target of your plan as you look back on your life. Success looks easy from the outside, but I will agree that every success I have achieved in my life was through hard work and tireless effort. When faced with tired less effort remember that it's your job to stay in control and keep grinding toward your goals. Somethings are just not going to come to you because you want to achieve it. You must go after it.

Chapter 6

IT'S YOUR GOD-GIVEN RIGHT

We all have things we believe in, things we want to accomplish. They are part of our destiny. Deep down we feel very strongly about accomplishing it, but when we hit setbacks, we tend to forget it. Let's say we did not get the promotion; our partner wants a divorce; we encounter a near death situation that traumatizes our life. Life has a way of putting our dreams down. However, they are buried under a lot of discouragement, past mistakes, rejections, failures, divorce, and negative voices. Why settle for mediocrity when you have all the potential buried inside of you. Even though you can sometimes give up on your dreams as I did, that does not mean that God gave up on your dreams. We have been through disappointments, but instead of remembering the hurt, the failures, what did or did not work, we should always strive to remember our dreams. We are given a dream in this world; this was our promise from God.

If you start believing again, regardless of the circumstances that you have been through, get your passion, have faith, God is going to bring forth your dream that was once dead. Stop letting your circumstances talk you out of it. You may not understand why something happens, why a family member walked away, an illness, or your business did not work. Every unfair situation, delay, and every close door is not a setback, it's a setup of an opportunity. Your dreams may take a long time, and you may not see how it can happen, but all it takes is one opportunity to come in your favor. Most of the time, we always remembered the disappointment of things that have happened in our life. Stop always remembering the negativity and turn it around to remember your dream. What is that gift, deep down inside you, what is that passion that others see and consistently compliment you on. What is that deep down inside that you used to get excited over. Do not ever think it is too late to follow your dream. I started chasing my dream at the age of 24. I waited to have almost died to realize the significance of me living out my callings. You do not have to wait, nor is it too late, too big and not possible. I never thought I could write a book, start my own business, or even finish my bachelor's degree and currently working on my speaking career. However, I made it all possible by having my dream and passion in front of me. Get your passion; there is still opportunity out there waiting for you. There are no such things as too many failures when it comes to your dream. You do not lack anything out of the ordinary; it is essential to change your perspective of your life.

When I was lying down in the hospital, when I had a seizure, God gave me a new perspective. God will always give you everything that you need to fulfill your gift. Nobody in this world can stop you; neither can disappointments, or loss. It's an old saying in the bible, "If God be for you, who can be against you." You have seeds of greatness deep beneath all those disappointments. One thing I realize, even though I had big dreams that I could not accomplish them by myself. I needed to depend on family, friends, and most importantly God. We all face challenges, but that does not mean that we should get discouraged. I fully understand now that when it comes to certain things, I will have faith and leave it to God. You can be all that you ought to be and accomplish all your dreams in this world. Whenever you come across disappointment, always remember your dreams. Stop believing in the lies that people are going to tell you.

I always believe that I had a seizure for a reason. Maybe you have an illness, or you have been dealing with an illness for a very long time. You decided to let that illness take over your life, so it has been several months, or even years and you have learned to live with it. Break out of that comfort zone, you have buried your dreams for too long, it is time that you fight back. Do not settle for the circumstances life has given you. Your dream is still in you, start believing again and firing back at your life. Stop thinking, it will never happen, I have had too many disappointments, and I am just adding more of it on it. I could have quickly settled for the life I was given when I had my seizures, but I realized that I will never let any circumstances stop me from chasing my dream. Start with changing your perspective of your life, just thank God that you are alive and pray if you are into religion. Continue to see the positivity in the situation because there is always negativity in every situation. Keep being patient and staying strong. Every day, look up and be grateful as your best days are in front of you. Remove any doubts, discouragement, and put faith forward.

I firmly believe that there are some dreams shut up in you, which is going to be burning with fire. Your destiny is calling you right now at this moment. You keep trying to brush it off, but it is time for you to continue it. You may have stumbled over the years but, do not ever give up. God wants all of us to be a dreamer that is why he empowered each one of us with a gift. Sometimes you are born from a family of poverty. We want to achieve and do something greater than what our family has done. When you get to a point in your life, and you continue to nurture what God has put in you, when you believe that you are destined to be great, it is important that you know everyone will not be happy.

When you have a dream, you are going to go through some downfalls. If you believe that you can overcome an illness, pay off your car, be successful besides some minor mistakes, start your business, then I believe you can achieve whatever it is that you want. As you are getting old, do not listen to the naysayers, critics, because nobody controls your destiny. The main individuals that are going to push your dreams down are your siblings, relatives, or immediate family. My only answer to you is, do not get distracted with fighting battles that would not matter in the next five years. You do not need anybody to believe in you. You do not require their approval. God has approved of your dreams, that is why he instills it in you. Just remember that your haters are going to hate you regardless. The best way to prove anyone that wishes bad upon you is to show the ability to keep getting better and pursuing your destiny.

Never forget that hater wants you to keep your dream buried in a dark place, so you don't rise higher and make them look bad. We all have dreams and goals in this world. If a person is jealous of you, it is because they have not realized their true potential yet. Successful people, people who have and pursue a dream, don't waste their time looking at what everybody else is doing. They are too busy chasing their destiny. Some people would not like you because you have a dream. They will try to convince you to continue working for somebody else, for the next 20 years, they will even try to convince you to bury your dream. If you are going to reach your full potential, you must make up your mind that you are in it for the long run, no matter how long it takes. You are not going to let circumstances discourage you, or let delays cause you to give up, or let insecure individual people get you distracted. Here is the key, continue to stay focused on your goal. You know you are going to be great when you have people opposing you. Understand that, if that dream weren't alive and right on track, you wouldn't have some many people against you. Just remember that you have the seeds of greatness, and nobody can take what God has bestowed in you. So, stop being depressed because the first few years of your life have been full of disappointment. Remember that you can do anything you set your mind. Never forget that DREAMER, know that nothing is impossible because they believe. They know that there will always be a way. God will always make a way.

Remember the promise you made your younger self. That Kid is still in you, and he is depending on you to make those dreams that you guys came up with. When you are a dreamer, life knows that you are capable of great things. There are going to be forces that are greater than anything you have ever imagined. Your mind will consistently try to convince you to settle where you are. Never forget that when you have huge setbacks they cannot stop your destiny; they are a sign that you're on the way to your destiny. Those disappointments did not happen to destroy your dream; it was all part of the process. Just remember to trust your process. The disappointment of people doing you wrong is just another step on your way to your destiny. After failing multiple exams in school, got rejected from Harvard 10 times, he was turned down from 30 jobs, was the only interviewee that was rejected from KFC, he was almost bankrupt when he started Alibaba. Eventually, he made it into a profitable company, and now Jack Ma is worth about 27.09 Billion. We all are all going to fail at something in our life but never give up when it comes to chasing your dreams and passion. As you keep going, you continue to give yourself a chance. Giving up is the greatest failure of all.

When God gives you a dream, that is a promise he has put in your heart, that doesn't mean it is going to come to pass without opposition, delays, and adversities. There will be things you do not understand. I never understood why God never allowed me to die when I had my seizures, while he allows me to have broken shoulders. I do believe he was not done with me yet. I had not fully fulfilled my dreams and goals yet. You will have plenty of opportunities to get discouraged and frustrated, thinking it is never going to happen. We are going to go through tough times; many great men in the bible and this world have done to always remember their dreams. You never came this far to finally quit, and give up on your dreams, life plans, family. You may not understand it, but God knows why he put in you that situation. As you are progressing through your life, he is directing your steps. Just remember to continue to do your part and have faith and keep going. After every disappointment in life, is a blessing. Your time is coming, obstacles are just detoured on the way to your destiny.

Your dream is not dead. When you face opposition, and things don't go your way, please recognize that the situation is not permanent. That situation is not your destination. Stop worrying about things that are only temporary. Stop pitying yourself. If you are not where you want to be right now, please understand, that is not your permanent home, it is just a temporary stop. This is just a phase that you are going through. So quite losing sleep and worrying yourself over a temporary stop. Stop being stressed over something that's not going to be permanent; it is only in your life for a season to teach you a lesson. I remember when I lived with my uncle in Philadelphia. He used to have me cut his grass during the summer, which I hated because I never like hard labor work growing up. I had always hated cutting grass, fixing cars, and any other jobs that required working with your hands. One thing I realized about winter in Philadelphia, the grass would look dead. Although, as I have grown up, I have come to realize that there is a season for everything. It is not that the grass is dead. I do not think it is the right season to blossom. You see that is the same when it comes to your life. We all are going to have our season. Some might last longer than they are intended to be. Every time I think about worrying about something. I ask myself, if it is something that I am going to care about five years down the road.

Are you letting an individual close to you steal and discourage your dreams? Stop letting people or things steal your joy because you think that you will never accomplish the goals and dreams that you have for yourself. Your dreams are not dead. Your time is coming. Please understand the right people, opportunities, career, vision and partners are all heading your way. You are probably on a detour right now, going through something that you do not understand, but it will all make sense in the future. Your dream has been buried deep down internally. You need to grab a shovel and shovel it out. It is easy to remember the disappointment, but I want you to always remember your dream. God promised you a dream and it is up to you to make it happen. When you are on the path you are destined to be on, you will rise higher, accomplish your goals, and become everything you were created to be.

Chapter 7

YOU WILL BECOME BETTER

A lot of times in life, we live to make our parents proud, family, and kids but continuously neglect to make ourselves proud. There are numerous reasons to make yourself proud; I will mention several different ways I believe that you can make yourself proud to continue having a fulfilling lifestyle. Following your passion, loving what you do, and not just viewing it as work will make you very proud. Before I decided to follow the dreams and goals that I have ever had for my life, I did not have any motivation to want to succeed. I mean really, want to succeed. I have always wanted to be successful, but I did not have a why. However, when I started to take a chance on my dreams and goals, which led me to follow my passion. Even though my passion is not the career field that I am currently in, I do love the fact that I can serve this country and still be able to do my passion. That is the greatest feeling anyone can ever have in my opinion. Whether you are looking to cultivate something you love as a professional stepping stone, as I am currently doing, or just extracurricular activities carry great benefits, or even if you do not have the burning desire passion that really stokes your flames, there is still hope for you too.

Doing things that you love and are proud of makes you feel good about yourself. It is crucial in the busy world that we live in to find time for yourself to greater happiness overall. Even a mother that had just had a baby needs sometimes to herself or else she will go crazy. I remember when my best friend had her daughter. She became very frustrated after several months taking care of the child. So therefore, my other best friend and I decided to give her a break from the child, so she can get back to her normal self. We all need some time by ourselves. Picture a time in your life where time almost has no meaning because you were so happy about what you were doing. The more you continue to do whatever that is, the better your life is going to feel. I know we are all busy. Whether it is that we are juggling demanding careers, family life or both. You make time for what is ESSENTIAL. While there are definitely moments we do not have time to spare. However most of us can make time depending on how you have looked.

When someone decides to offer you 1 million or 1 billion. I can almost guarantee that you are going to make time to get that money, I know I would. So, in conclusion, we will always make time for what is important or what we deem as priority.

"You can only grow if you are willing to feel awkward and uncomfortable when you try something new" – Brian Tracy.

Stop living your life in your comfort zone. Nothing great comes out of your life, living in your comfort zone. You may be feeling uninspired, emotionally drained, and lack direction. As the old saying goes, "When life tosses you lemon, go ahead and make lemonade." From time to time, you may have a period of uncertainty, which on the surface appears as though the world is sinking. Please understand that every effort, every step, and every failure draws you closer to your goals, dreams which will make you proud in the end. I do not believe any effort goes in vain on your journey to success. Most successful entrepreneurs require the confidence of never giving up on their plan, goals, vision, even when the forces are against them.

I highly encourage anybody reading this book to adopt the philosophy that it is imperative to step out of your comfort zone. Success does not lie where things are easy.

The real fruits of success in life are being uncomfortable. You must be willing to take risks, whether big or small, and to gradually move in the direction of your dreams and goals. Your belief system will trigger the power for you to do things. Being familiar with things and always playing it safe, often time will keep you stagnant. Do not be content with just sailing through life you will never reach your true potential like that. Just because you did not achieve your goals the way you wanted does not make you a failure. Tony Robbins said, "Success leaves clues." If you keep stepping out of your comfort zone, you will continue to get better at your personal life. Every successful person has pushed past their comfort zone to reach their current level of success. They all had to overcome certain things to create a new way of life and to pave the way for others to follow in their footsteps. Never forget that learning and growing from failures will help drive you past your comfort zone.

Knowing what your weakness and strength is one of the most important things you could do in your life. A lot of people going through life have no idea of what they are good at, so they spend the rest of their life continuing to do things that they believe that they are good at. Although they may never be great at that thing they settle and think that they are just average. If you are reading this book. I believe that you have a gift, greatness in you. There is something out there that only you are good at, and nobody can compare. Stop focusing on your weakness and focus more of your energy on your strength. Take time out of your day to continue to improve your strength because only in your strength lies your true potential. A lot of successful people have told me the key to their success is to focus on your strength, not weakness. I guaranteed that Warren Buffet, Bill Clinton, Bill Gates, Oprah Winfrey all had weaknesses, but they definitely didn't achieve their success by focusing on them.

You are going to suck at something that is part of life. Nobody is going to be good at everything; let's just make that clear. Look at Michael Jordan, when he retired from basketball to go and play baseball. He was not as effective in baseball as he was in basketball. Basketball came naturally to him. MJ realized that his strength was basketball, therefore he came back into the league and continued to achieve a huge amount of success. Imagine if he would have stayed in baseball and continue to work on his skills as a baseball player. I don't think he would have been the icon he is today in baseball as he is in basketball. Now take a long time in your life. Most of us tend to complain and grumble at some of the things that we are not good at in our life. I want you to take a moment today to think about all the things that you are good at naturally and focus on working on them until you become great at it.

Wanting to become a millionaire, drive a particular car, own a specific house are all good things to dream of or have but if your goals and your plans are not clear as I mentioned in the previous chapter, then you would not achieve any of those things to fully make yourself proud. I firmly believe that you must truly commit to claiming happiness and success in your life. When you are so used to seeing the world full of doubts it is a little hard, but you must shift your mindset and instead of seeing problems, you become so positive that you lose yourself in all the criticism that people tell you. Every day as I continue to live on this earth I find that having been given a second chance from God with my seizure incident that left me nearly dead, my peace and blessings are not so hard to come, so I do not need to focus on positivity because that is who I am now.

I have reached a point in this life that I am so convinced that God only brings you problems to show you what your energy can get you through. I had to fully experience that to understand it, which has led me to help more people than I thought I could. When you see yourself as a service to others and make a decision to not only help them in their life, this is not only a rewarding feeling, but it also sets you apart from others around the world. I highly believe as you continue to help other people, you will be hugely rewarded, whether it is in money, cars, clothes, jewelry, etc.

A lot of times, we look at our circumstances and struggle and we do not know how we are going to get through it. Please understand that things won't happen to us; they happen for us. My seizure changed the course of my destiny. When you understand that your struggle is what is going to make you into the person that you are meant to be, then you will be jovial about the situation. While looking at our struggle that way makes the situation a little bit easier to find opportunity in any situation that we experienced in life. I believe our struggle is a friendly reminder that yes, we have been through a lot, but if we keep doing amazing and great things, while being persistent of our potential can show us so much more. So, if you have hit a road bump at this point of your life, do not stop, slowly go over it and keep moving toward your target goals and dreams.

When I made the decision that I was going to chase my dream of being a professional speaker, I spent a lot of time on working and improving myself. On the road to success, you must fully find and understand who you are from the core; you have to develop specific routines, values and belief systems that will take you from where you are to where you need to be. I knew that I could continue to get better, while appreciating the individuals around me for exactly who they are. While I genuinely appreciate people for all their beauties and imperfection, it allowed me to work on myself with the same appreciation. Nobody in this life is perfect, yet we find ourselves loving those with some of the worst flaws. So why is it that we do not love ourselves, with all our imperfections. This question was at the top of my mind for several months, until I started reading and learning how to appreciate myself for all my flaws. While I continued to enjoy all the things around me, I found out that if I continue to work on myself, the more I will appreciate the people around me. Stop being hard on yourself all the time; it's okay to make mistakes but continue to work and become a better you for tomorrow. I want you to know that you are meant so much more than you are today, but only in this moment, you are the perfect you.

Why else should you decide to become a better you? Is it because you want to prove yourself to the world, prove yourself in your field of career, or prove yourself to your relationships with different individuals? You will never know your true potential, who you can give value to, help grow, inspire, that will give you an opportunity in the future, or even introduce you to someone that is willing to hire individuals in your field of work. I have committed myself for the rest of my life to always be willing to give people value, because what we give, eventually we will receive it in one form. I am not saying that you should give because you expect something in return but give and help others because you know that God has blessed you with a lot or just enough that you have the privilege to be able to even consider it. A lot of times when I help people, I do not expect anything back, I made a commitment to always be of service to people. That is the number one reason why I decided to join the service. I always want to be of value to everyone I encounter.

So, are you going to decide to live your life to the fullest or play the role of a victim? Only you have control over the quality of life that you believe that you deserve. Only you can make that choice and nobody else can make that for you. You can design the lifestyle that you want, so stop wasting your time on things that are irrelevant and would not matter in five year and concentrate on continuing to improve yourself. Whatever in this life that you desire, you must decide to become a different or better person to receive it. There are numerous different ways to become successful, but what if you find success and you are not proud of the person you have become. In a world full of sin, drugs, sickness, war, poverty, etc. It is not easy to have positivity but if you strive to provide service to others instead of just doing things because of money, giving to others instead of always expecting and most importantly appreciating people, for who they are, you will make a lot easy on yourself. At the end of the day it all comes down to something we have always been blessed with and some of us have been fortunate to have, which is you still have the power of choice. What you choose to do with it, determines how far you will go in your life and how prosperous your life will become. I have decided to live a positive life, understand struggles, bad breaks and circumstances are going to come, but through it all I will always think positive in every situation.

PILLAR #3

Chapter 8

YOU ONLY LIVE ONCE

Where does your inspiration come from? Is it internal, external, or even materialist? Well, I would like to tell you my inspiration comes from my God, my families, friends, struggles, disappointments and those that have helped me along my journey of success. I am the oldest of all the kids from my mother and father. I am inspired by how I can go to America as a refugee and I witness my mother transform from being dependent on our father to being a single mother of four boys and one girl. I observed her going through a lot of things in her life, but she stayed strong and kept on pushing and not giving up. I remember when she worked her whole pregnancy with my last brother, who ended up coming early. I thought I was going to lose my mother, I did not know what to expect because they told her that she had to have my brother. I will never forget when she called me and said that she was going through labor. That was one of the saddest days of my life as a young man because I did not know what to expect. One moment, I was cleaning up the house with my mother and the next she called me to tell me that she is going into labor. Do you know what is like to see your mother be in pain?

For a young teenager that was a very hard situation. Although my mother and I do not see eye to eye on a lot of things, I look up to her a lot when it comes to believing and having faith. I will never forget; I could not help her during her pregnancy because nobody would hire me. I searched everywhere for a job, they would say that I needed work experience which I did not have at that time. I have seen my mother through her struggles and seen her at her happiest. As many times I have watched my mother go through disappointments, which I could not do anything at that time. Today, I get to watch my mother testify and preach the word of God as she has followed her calling. We only live once in this life, it is vital to understand that no matter what you are going through in this life, there is always something that demands your presence.

Life is short, and our days are very numbered. The life expectancy of the average human being is about 80 years old, and a lot of us do not even make it to see 80. That is why it baffles me when I see someone that is young complaining about how their life sucks and they hate it and cannot do anything about it. We all have a vision of what we want to do in this world, the same vision that is in our mind is no different than a seed planted in the ground. Of course, in the initial stages of your life you will not be able to see what your true potential is, but that does not mean to stop working on your goals. Although your vision will take time for it to sprout, never stop watering it. As you embark on this journey of greatness it will be hard for others to see what you have in your mind, but never stop working. Never stop grinding, and if you keep taking days off; you are only prolonging your process. The best way to show how valuable your life is or have been is to keep investing in yourself every day and believe that you are going to succeed no matter what the circumstances so that you can wake up, living in your dream.

If you are going to die regardless of what you do, why is it that a lot of us on this earth spend our lives doing something we do not love. It's time to decide to go for what it is that you love. But first, you must understand that success begins in the mind. Most of the successful people know their destination will come with patience. Learning how to master patience and the lifestyle of successful individuals before you even receive any physical reward. When I realized that tomorrow's was not promised, I made sure that every day I gave it my all to whatever task that I had at hand. When you decide what it is that you want to be with your life, then determine when do you want to become this individual or want to achieve it and keep on grinding and in due time you will accomplish what you have always wanted, when you go after what you want in life the stars align. It does not matter where you start or how you start the only requirement is that you never end once you start. There is a psychological effect in being consistent, which will tell you that once your mind has emerged for several hours on something, your mind will detect things that the untrained eye cannot see.

The more wisdom you have, the more of the unseen become seen, which is going to translate to you becoming more powerful than you were before. Successful people fail; to prevail, they trust their process and act on their vision. They refuse to settle because they understand that they deserve the lifestyle that they want. They continue to focus on one thing, while making it a priority and sticking with the goal or vision. Your life is not going to continue to get easier as you go through your struggles, the only difference is that you will continue to get used to life. You will either get stronger or regress. A lot of the big companies right now have had a small beginning, so you need to understand that, just because you come from a small background does not mean you are not better than the individuals that are different from you. We all have a seed of greatness deep inside us, but we will have to give birth to our dream. While in college, I came across the movie "Limitless," which has Bradley Cooper as the main character. In the movie it just basically talks about how the average person uses less than ten percent of his or her mind, which means that ninety percent of the mind's capability is not being used. The goals are to try and use at least ten percent of your brain. Like I said in the earlier picture, God created gifts for everyone. Only in your Gifts you were meant to excel. You do not have a limit on how high you can grow.

You must believe that we all have what it takes. You must believe that you have a gift, diamond, treasure inside you. People will try to push it down, circumstances may have changed your outlook-on life. Maybe you have tried to succeed multiple times already and you keep hitting brick walls. I will tell you to continue growing, if you are not buried 6 feet, you must keep trying, again, again and hope. Maybe you have been told a thousand times, "no" when it comes to doing what you love or following your dream, but I want you to keep asking until you get the "yes" that you have been waiting to hear. You have got to keep pressing. Too many people grow satisfied with far less than what they are meant. Most of the time is discouragement, but all seriousness they simply get comfortable. They stop reaching for it and lose faith. Most of the reason is a lot of people do not understand the potential they have inside. Our potential has been put in us when we were born, whether we use it or not it does not diminish but it only impacts our future. I used to think that my past reduces my potential, but I have come to an understanding that it is not where you are or where you have been, but it is where you are going.

The past never reduces your potential. It is okay if you didn't grow up with your mother, father, family, or even in a shelter home. The most significant part of all that is those situations does not change your potential. I always used to think, by my uncle not believing, I would never achieve any amount of success. However, the key to any success is YOU. Your disappointment, life-changing events you have been through, does not affect your potential. When you tap into your faith, that is when you will rise higher. You have all the capabilities that you need to succeed.

When I was in the hospital while waiting for the nurse to bring me food, I used to ask myself this question "Are you willing to break free from your self-imposed limitation and start stretching to the next level of life." We allow our experiences from the past to keep us from pressing forward. We live in an era where we seek the approvals of others. Before we decide to do anything, we focus on the approval of our business partner, family, friends, or spouse. Do not allow other people to talk you out of your dreams. Saying things like "You do not have what it takes," "Your English is not very good," or "I do not think you will ever be successful."

I knew a guy when I worked for G4S Secure solution, he told me that he got a position where he could talk to Officer over the radio in the control room center, and a lot of Officer complain that they could not hear him, so they took him out of the office job and put him at the gate. He realized that, for him to become successful, it was not going to be at G4S, he decided to finish his school. Now he works at an IT company getting paid a good salary and is currently married with children. You as an adult must realize whether you can fully grow in an environment. I see so many people working for a company for almost 20 years or more and are still at the same position. The point of life is to continue growing.

Who told you that you don't have what it takes to succeed? Who told you that if you failed at school you would not make it in the world? Who told you that you are not good looking enough to marry the person of your dream? Who told you that you are a Cs student rather than an A's student? Who told you that something was wrong with you?

These are lies that other's tell people, and they grow up believing it for the rest of their life. Stop looking at what you lack and start believing that all things are possible. I have never dreamt of being in the military, but I am blessed to have joined. For several years my mother tried to get me to join, I had no desire. I used to let my fear of the unknown control me. Until one day, I decided that I was going to stop letting my fears control me. We all have fears and weaknesses, but chasing your dream will take you places you have never imagined. The key is to get your eyes from focusing on your problem, fears and focus on what ought to be, and take a step of faith. Keep focusing on where you are going, so you will always have your eyes fixed on where you want to be. It's the main reason why some people failed to succeed. They focus on their hurt and pains. They are living in self-pity and complaining that life is not fair. The key is to keep rising higher to where you want to go.

When I was in high school, I remember I tried out for the soccer team freshman year and I did not make the starting lineup. Although, I never thought I would ever make the team, instead I kept a positive vision and asked the coach if he can help me develop my game during the summer. Which resulted in me starting my sophomore year. Other people do not determine your potential. Do not let negative words or attitudes take root and keep you from pressing forward. God did not give you a dream to not fulfill it. You have all the tools that you need for you to succeed. I dare you to take a step of faith you will discover gifts inside that you never realized were there. Stop missing the great opportunities that you have in store for your life by letting people talk you out of it.

Always keep stretching to the next level of your life because you only get one life. When disappointment and rejection knock you down, get back up, and go again. We give up too easily on our dreams. We need to understand that God has given each one of us a gift from birth, and as you continue to improve your life from dead-end, still do not give up. Always find a different route. Stop making the same mistakes and settling to where you are. When one door closes, go look for another door. The dream that you have burning inside of you might be bigger than the current situation. Throughout life, we are never always going to understand everything that happens along the way. But we have to learn to trust our process and what God has for us. We have got to believe that if we keep pressing, our life will get to where we need to be. You must let go of your disappointments, because you cannot change the past, but you can do something about the future. When you focus on where you are headed it is more significant than where you are from or what is happening. Stop looking back. We all have something to offer that nobody else does. Maybe you may have had a more difficult or been through several near-death situations. But do not give up. Never go around thinking you have reached your limit. Do not start limiting your thinking, saying that you have gone as far as possible. Remember if you do not like what you are doing or you do not like the direction that you are going. Only you have the power to change that. If you do not have any support system, or nobody to encourage you. Learn to motivate yourself. Keep pressing and continue to give your dreams a chance. Every day as you wake up, tell yourself positive declarations and continue to remind yourself of how great you are. You were not meant to be average; you were made to excel. You were created to leave your mark on this great generation. Learn to discipline your thoughts to stop thinking negative. Learn to quit mourning over something you cannot change. Learn to leave that close door and step into a different one in front of you. Learn to stop giving up easily. Learn to stay in a healthy environment because your full potential is when you put yourself in an environment where you can grow or those around you want to see you grow. Stop hanging out with negative people and be expecting to have a positive lifestyle. Always beware of negative influences as you pursue your dreams. People will always have something negative to say about you when you become a dreamer. Our life is too short for us to be pulled down by the negatives of others. It does not matter how great your potential or gift is, you will never really flourish in an environment like that. Always remember to tell yourself that "you have come too far to stop now and that you are a victor instead of a victim."

MY ACKNOWLEDGMENT

I want to thank God for everything that he has done in my life. Whether it was good or bad, I know that everything was for good. He has blessed my life tremendously, and he continues to add favor and value to my life. I will forever be grateful to him. I want to thank my mother Clara, for being a strong, beautiful woman, as she led the foundation of how a woman is supposed to be in my life. Although we do not see eye to eye to a lot of things, Mom, I will forever love you, and nobody will ever take your place in my heart. I want to thank my brother Ibraham for helping take care of me doing the time I had my seizure. I love you, brother. I wish nothing but the best for you in all your future endeavors. I want to thank my little brother Kelity for always making me smile during my down time. Kelity you will always be my first son. I love you to the end of time little brother. I would like to thank Trevor. Trevor, you have been more than a father in my life and I could not be more grateful for you as you took care of me during my time of need more than anybody could ever have. I will always love you. I would like to thank my Sister Samantha and Brother Adrian. You guys have been the best friend a person could ever ask for. You guys were in my corner when I needed you guys. You are more than a friend to me. I will forever love you all. I would like to thank my brother Evan. I love you bro. You have been a tremendous help to me when nobody would offer any help when I first came to Virginia. I would like to thank my ex, Tasha. You have been a force in my life since day one. Always pushing me to be the very best man that I could be. God bless you and I wish you all the best this life has to offer.

CONCLUSION

I hope that you have gained some type of inspiration from reading my book and you can use this to apply toward your life. I believe we are living in the best time of the world right now, and I would like you to take the opportunity to allow me to coach you on how to train your mind to live your calling.

I want to do the best I can to ensure that everyone in this life is living in their calling. You do not need to wait until you have money. All you need is to believe.

Please send me an email, I would Love to hear from you:

lusene718@gmail.com

I hope you will allow me to coach you towards achieving massive success.

###

ABOUT THE AUTHOR

Lusene Donzo was born in Monrovia, Liberia, raised in several different countries, West Africa. He later came to the U.S as a refuge, because of the war that was in Ivory Coast. Lusene has been in the military for about six years. From Private to now as a First Lieutenant. Lusene Donzo is the owner of Lusene Donzo and Association. Lusene Donzo and Association is a Speaking Company that Lusene founded.

Lusene Donzo is an Army Officer, Speaker, Author and a graduate of the Historical Black College University, Virginia State University. He received his Bachelor in Computer Science and Military Science and is planning getting his Masters in Public Relations in Advance and Corporate Communication. He is currently on Active Duty as an Artillery Officer. He is very active in the community as is determined to help positively impact the Youth. His desire is to empower people to thrive in life and overcome obstacles.